30119 023 607 205

THE NAXOS BOOK OF
CAROLS

24 CAROLS FOR ADVENT AND CHRISTMAS
SATB (ORGAN)

ANTONY PITTS

D1612991

NAXOS

FABER *ff* MUSIC

Faber Music Ltd – 3 Queen Square – London
in association with
Select Music Ltd – 3 Wells Place – Redhill – Surrey

© 2004 by Faber Music Ltd
First published in 2004 by Faber Music Ltd and Select Music Ltd
Faber Music 3 Queen Square London WC1N 3AU
Select Music Ltd 3 Wells Place Redhill Surrey
Cover design © 2004 by Select Music Ltd
Original CD cover design artwork by QD London, to a concept by Philippa Green
Book jacket cover design by Matthew Lee
Music processed by Jackie Leigh
Printed in England by Caligraving Ltd
All rights reserved

ISBN 0-571-52325-0

To buy Faber Music publications or to find out about the full range of titles available
please contact your local music retailer or Faber Music sales enquiries:

Faber Music Limited, Burnt Mill, Elizabeth Way, Harlow, CM20 2HX England
Tel: +44 (0)1279 82 89 82   Fax: +44 (0)1279 82 89 83
sales@fabermusic.com   fabermusic.com

CONTENTS

The hope

The message

The baby

The King of kings

total timing:
78'59"

All arrangements/realisations by Antony Pitts

THE COMPOSER

Antony Pitts was born in 1969 and was a treble in the Chapel Royal, Hampton Court Palace and an Academic Scholar at New College, Oxford; he is now a Senior Producer at BBC Radio 3. Antony began composing at an early age; in the last few years his music has been premièred in Wigmore Hall in London, the Concertgebouw in Amsterdam, and the Philharmonie Kammermusiksaal in Berlin. He has recently written pieces for the Berlin Radio Choir, Cambridge Voices, the Clerks' Group, the Choir of Westminster Cathedral, the London Festival of Contemporary Church Music, Oxford Camerata, Schola Cantorum of Oxford, and the Swingle Singers.

Other choral works published by Faber Music:

Adoro te (SATB divisi)	0-571-52083-9
Libera me/Lamentations V (SATB divisi)	0-571-51830-3
XL (40-part motet)	0-571-54040-6

THE CD RECORDING

(NAXOS 8.557330 – THE NAXOS BOOK OF CAROLS – TONUS PEREGRINUS/ANTONY PITTS)

The ensemble TONUS PEREGRINUS was founded at New College, Oxford in 1990. The name *tonus peregrinus* comes from an ancient psalm tone: the 'wandering tone'. The ensemble won a Cannes Classical Award (2004) for its chart-topping debut disc of Arvo Pärt's *Passio* (Naxos 8.555860) and critical acclaim for *The Mass of Tournai* – the earliest complete polyphonic Mass and Passion settings (Naxos 8.555861). Other releases include *Organum from Notre-Dame* (Naxos 8.557340), *Sweet Harmony* – masses & motets by John Dunstaple (Naxos 8.557341), and the first-ever opera *Le Jeu de Robin et Marion* by Adam de la Halle (Naxos 8.557337).

TONUS PEREGRINUS
Sopranos: Joanna Forbes, Rebecca Hickey
Altos: Kathryn Oswald, Alexander L'Estrange
Tenors: Richard Eteson, Alexander Hickey
Basses: Francis Brett, Simon Grant
Organ: Nicholas Chalmers
Director: Antony Pitts
www.tonusperegrinus.co.uk

℗ 2003 & © 2003 Naxos Rights International Ltd
24-bit recording made 28–29 July 2003
in St Jude-on-the-hill, Hampstead Garden Suburb, London, UK
engineered by Geoff Miles
produced by Jeremy Summerly
edited by Antony Pitts

FOREWORD

The Naxos Book of Carols is both very old and very new: a collection of carols drawing on centuries of tradition, but in new arrangements specially commissioned by the record label Naxos. Every generation musicians have added something of their own to the yearly festivities of Christmas, and even those age-old tunes and words which have stood the test of time have also been weathered by it: carols are part of a living ritual that is not concerned so much with authenticity as with sincerity. Here the selection ranges from the most well-known of all to some less familiar mediaeval carols as well as entirely original music, including my younger brother John Pitts's take on O little town of Bethlehem. The arrangements themselves are sometimes a very light touch on what is known and loved, and sometimes a complete rethink of a traditional carol. In the case of *The Holly and the Ivy*, the rarely-heard tune was transcribed from a tape in the BBC's archives and is intertwined with the 'common or garden' melody for the same words.

The 24 carols tell the Christmas story in the same way that an Advent calendar gradually opens its windows day by day through December. The carols are grouped in four sections, each focusing on a different part of the narrative: the Advent hope and expectancy of the coming Messiah, the message of the angel Gabriel to the virgin Mary and then of the angels to the shepherds some nine months later, the baby in the familiar but extraordinary manger-birth scene, and finally the visit of the wise men and ultimately 'all nations' to adore the King of kings. Each of the four sections is capped by a rousing hymn/carol which follows the customary alternation of unaccompanied verses, descants and colourful last-verse harmony.

The arrangements are designed, on the whole, for use by choir and/or congregation – it should be possible to sing along with the tune in each verse, whatever else is happening – and the accompaniments are suited as much to church organ as to the piano or keyboard at home, at school or in the pub. The choral settings are mostly in the standard four parts: soprano, alto, tenor and bass; depending on circumstances, vocal parts may be doubled or replaced by instruments. Although the eponymous CD is a (very) reliable guide to tempi and dynamics, these are not the only possible interpretations. A spirit of freedom and joy pervaded the composition of these arrangements, and I hope this will come across whenever and wherever these carols are sung and played.

This carol-book is dedicated to my four children – Thomas, Anna, Raphael, Sophia – who may also come to love these carols and their message of hope: the baby born in Bethlehem two thousand years ago is the coming King whose 'Name shall stand for ever'.

Antony Pitts, April 2004

1. O come, o come, Emmanuel

(after Advent 'O' Antiphons)
John M. Neale, Antony Pitts

?13TH-CENTURY
arranged Antony Pitts

May be sung processionally, with or without organ/instrumental accompaniment to keep pitch; organ compulsory for last verse; verses – including the opening Latin verse – may be omitted as necessary.

come to thee, O Is - ra - el.

come to thee, O Is - ra - el.

thee, O Is - ra - el.

2. O come, A - do - nai, sov - 'reign

come to thee, O Is - ra - el.

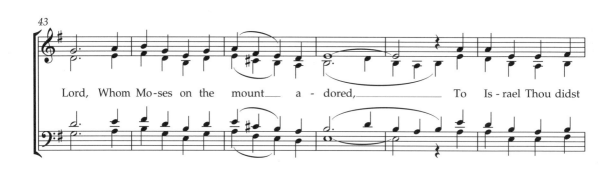

Lord, Whom Mo - ses on the mount a - dored, To Is - rael Thou didst

give the Law in cloud, and ma - jes - ty and awe. Re - joice! re -

- joice! Em - ma - nu - el shall come to thee, O Is - ra - el.

- joice! Em - ma - nu - el shall come to thee, O Is - ra - el.

- joice! Em - ma - nu - el shall come to thee, O Is - ra - el.

- joice! Em - ma - nu - el shall come to thee, O Is - ra - el.

from_____ his chain. Re - joice! re - joice! Em - ma - nu -

from_____ his chain. Re - joice!_____ re - joice! Em - ma - nu -

from_____ his chain. Re - joice!_____ re - joice!__ Em - ma - nu -

from_____ his chain. Re - joice! re - joice! Em - ma - nu -

- el shall come to thee, O Is - ra - el. 5. O come, Thou Day-spring

- el shall__ come to thee, Is - ra - el. 5. O come, Thou Day-spring

- el shall__ come to thee, Is - ra - el. 5. O come, Thou Day-spring

- el_____ shall__ come to thee, Is - ra - el. 5. O come, Thou Day-spring

14

6. O come, Thou King of na - tions, come,— Thou Cor - ner - stone, Which

But_____

ma - kest one;_____ But dust and ash - es at_____ Thy

ma - kest one;_____ But__

feet,— now raise us to Thy mer - cy - seat.— Re - joice!— re - joice! Em-

mer - cy - seat. Re - joice! re - joice! Em-

- ma - nu - el shall come to thee, O Is - ra - el._____

- ma - nu - el shall come to thee,— O__ Is - ra - el.

- ma - nu - el shall come to thee, O Is - ra - el.

7. O come, O come, Em - ma - nu - el, And ran - som cap - tive Is - ra - el,_____ That mourns in lone - ly e - xile here Un - til the Son of God____ ap - pear. Re - joice! re - joice! Em - ma - nu - el shall come to thee, O Is - ra - el.

2. Of the Father's heart begotten

(after Prudentius)
John M. Neale, Henry Baker & Antony Pitts

PIAE CANTIONES, 1582
arranged Antony Pitts

Verses may be sung alternately by congregation and choir alone – for each verse, the main tune begins at the double barline;
verse 5 harmony may be used throughout; two additional verses may be used before verse 7 (9).

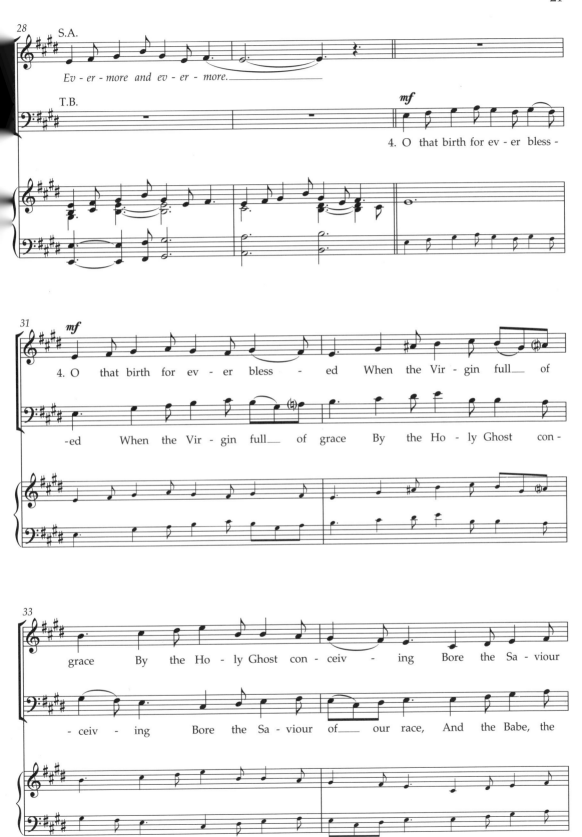

43

God— and King, Let no tongue on earth be si - - - lent:

45

Ev - 'ry voice in con - cert ring: *Ev - er - more and ev - er - more.*___

47 S. *mp*

6. This is He whom seer and si - byl Chant - ed of with one— ac -

A.

T.

B.

6. This is He whom seer and si -

Optional verses

7. Hail, Great Judge of souls departed,
   Hail, Great King of ev'ry land,
   To the Father's Throne ascended,
   With a shout from His right hand
   Thou shalt come and bring Thy justice:
   Evil shall no longer stand
   Evermore and evermore.
   (sung to v.5)

8. Old and young men join in chorus,
   Lips of infants bring Thee praise,
   Mothers, maidens, raise your voices,
   Sing in joy for endless days,
   May the righteous song resounding
   Echo our harmonious lays
   Evermore and evermore.
   (sung to v.6)

3. O quickly come

Laurence Tuttiett

ANTONY PITTS

May be sung with or without organ/instrumental accompaniment. Dynamics are left to the choir's discretion.

14

clouds dis-solve when Thou art____ near.
make Thy scat - tered peo - ple____ one.

____ dis - solve when__ Thou__ art____ near.
____ Thy scat - tered__ peo - ple____ one.

clouds dis-solve_ when Thou art____ near.____
make Thy scat - tered peo - ple____ one.____

clouds____ dis-solve when Thou____ art near.
make____ Thy scat - tered peo - - ple one.

17

3. O quick - ly come, true Life of all! For death is migh - ty
4. O quick - ly come, sure Light of all! And drive the gloom - y
5. O Bless - ed Sa - viour, Love of Love! O Fa - ther, Fount of

3. O quick - ly come, true Life of all!____ For death is migh-ty
4. O quick - ly come, sure Light of all!____ And drive the gloom-y
5. O Bless - ed Sa - viour, Love of Love!____ O Fa - ther, Fount of

3. O__ quick - ly come, true_ Life of all! For death is migh - ty
4. O__ quick - ly come, sure_ Light of all! And drive the gloom - y
5. O__ Bless - ed Sa - viour, Love of Love! O Fa - ther, Fount of

3. O quick - ly come, true_ Life of all! For death is migh - ty
4. O quick - ly come, sure_ Light of all! And drive the gloom - y
5. O Bless - ed Sa - viour, Love of Love! O Fa - ther, Fount of

4. Verbum Patris umanatur, O, O

Anon. (?13th-Century)

?13TH-CENTURY
arranged Antony Pitts

Upper and lower voices/instruments may be spatially separated.

5. Lo! He comes

(after John Cennick)
Charles Wesley

THOMAS OLIVERS, MARTIN MADAN
arranged Antony Pitts

Verse 2 may be sung unaccompanied; last verse unison.

40

6. The holly and the ivy

Trad. collected Cecil J. Sharp & Antony Pitts

collected CECIL J. SHARP & ANTONY PITTS
arranged Antony Pitts

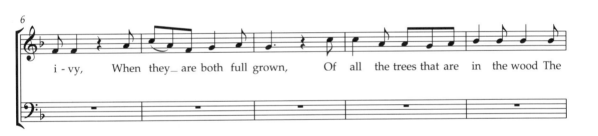

This carol is particularly suited to accompaniment on the piano. Dynamics are left to the choir's discretion.

42

53

4. The hol - ly bears _ a pri-ckle As sharp _ as a - ny thorn, And

4. The hol - ly bears _ a pri-ckle As sharp _ as a - ny thorn, And

57

Ma - ry bore _ sweet Je - sus Christ On Christ - mas Day in the morn. *The*

Ma - ry bore _ sweet Je - sus Christ On Christ - mas Day in the morn. *The*

61

ris - ing of___ the sun,_____ And the run - ning of___ the deer, The___

ris - ing of___ the sun,_____ And the run - ning of___ the deer, The___

play - ing of__ the mer-ry or - gan,__ Sweet sing-ing all in__ the choir.

play - ing of__ the mer-ry or - gan,__ Sweet sing-ing all in__ the choir.

6. The hol - ly and_ the i - vy When they_ are both full grown Of

6. The hol-ly and_ the i - vy__ When they are both_ full grown Of__

all the trees that are in the wood The hol - ly bears_ the crown.__

all the trees_ that are in the wood_ The_ hol-ly bears_ the crown.__

7. Lo, there a Rose is blooming
(*Es ist ein Roess entsprungen*)

(after German)
Antony Pitts, John M. Neale

?PRAETORIUS
arranged Antony Pitts

Optional repeat of verse 1 (instrumental) at end.

48

8. Alleluya - A new work

Anon. (15th-Century)
adapted Antony Pitts

ANON. (ENGLISH, 15TH-CENTURY)
arranged Antony Pitts

Solo or unison; begin with either refrain or verse 1; optional verse 4

54

Al - le - lu - - - - - - ya!

lower voice(s)

upper voice(s)

1. A new___ work_ is__ close___ at__ hand,___   A
2. By Ga - bri - el___ be - gun___ it___ was,___   By
3. Now is__ ful - fill'd__ the pro - phe - cy,___   Now
4. Al - le - lu - ya___ this_ sweet - est__ song,___   Al -

new_____ work____ is__ close_____ at__ hand_____ Through
Ga - bri - el_____ be - gun_____ it__ was_____ Just
is__ ful - fill'd___ the_ pro - phe - cy_____ Of
-le - lu - ya_____ this_ sweet - est__ song_____ Out

might and__ grace of God's_____ own_ Son,_____ Through
as the__ sun shone through_____ the__ glass,_____ Just
Da - vid___ and of Je - re - my,_____ Of
of the__ green - est branch____ it__ sprung,_____ Out

9. Ding! dong! merrily on high

G.R. Woodward

JEHAN TABOUROT
arranged Antony Pitts

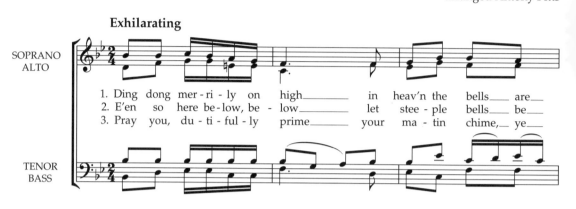

1. Ding dong mer-ri-ly on high in heav'n the bells are
2. E'en so here be-low, be-low let stee-ple bells be
3. Pray you, du-ti-ful-ly prime your ma-tin chime, ye

ring - ing, Ding dong ve-ri-ly the sky is
swung - en, And I - O, I - O, I - O by
ring - ers; May you beau-ti-ful-ly rhyme your

ring - - ing,
swung - - en,
ring - - ers;

riv'n with an - gels sing - ing:
priest and peo - ple sung - en: *Glo* - - -
eve - time song, ye sing - ers:

May be sung in harmony or unison with brass and other instrumental accompaniment.

10. While shepherds watched

Nahum Tate(?)

?CHRISTOPHER TYE, GEORGE KIRBYE
arranged Antony Pitts

Verse 4 or verse 6 harmony may be used throughout as appropriate.

11. The Song of Angels

(Hymnes and Songs of the Church - Song 34)

Anon.

ORLANDO GIBBONS
arranged Antony Pitts

Any of the three versions – melody alone, melody and bass, 4-part harmony – may be used.

Thus An - gels sung, and thus___ sing___ we; To

God on high all glo - ry be:

God on high___ all___ glo - ry be:
God___ on high___ all_____ glo - ry be: Let

God on high all glo - ry be:

His Peace be - stowe,

Him___ on___ Earth___ His Peace___ be - stowe, And___
His___ Peace___ be - stowe,

His Peace___ be - stowe,

His fa - vour show.

un - to___ men___ His___ fa - vour___ show.
His___ fa - vour___ show.

His fa - vour show.

12. Hark! the herald angels sing

Charles Wesley
adapted George Whitefield, Martin Madan

FELIX MENDELSSOHN
arranged Antony Pitts

1. Hark! the he - rald an - gels sing: Glo - ry to the new-born King!
2. Christ, by high - est heav'n a - dored, Christ the ev - er - last - ing Lord!

Peace on earth and mer - cy mild, God and sin - ners re - con - ciled.
Late in time be - hold Him come, Off - spring of a vir - gin's womb.

Joy - ful, all ye na - tions, rise, Join the tri - umph of the skies;
Veiled in flesh the God - head see, Hail th'in-car - nate De - i - ty!

With th'an - ge - lic host pro - claim: Christ is born in Beth - le - hem.
Pleased, as Man, with man to dwell, Je - sus, our Em - man - nu - el.

Verse 2 may be sung unaccompanied; last verse descant may be doubled on trumpets.

to the

Hark! the he - rald__ an - gels__ sing: Glo - ry__ to the new - born King!

to__ the

DESCANT

3. Hail! the heav'n - born Prince of Peace! Hail! the__ Sun of Righ - teous-ness!

UNISON

3. Hail! the heav'n - born Prince of Peace!__ Hail! the Sun of Righ - teous - ness!

Light and__ life__ to__ all He brings,__ Risen with heal - ing in__ His__wings.

Light and life to all He brings,__ Risen with heal - ing in His wings.

13. Silent night

(after Joseph Mohr)
John F. Young

FRANZ XAVER GRUBER
arranged Antony Pitts

Optional verse 2 tenor solo which may be improvised/embellished while other voices hum. See guideline solo on page 69.

68

10

peace,_____ Sleep_ in hea - ven-ly peace.
born!_____ Christ_ the Sa - viour is born!
birth!_____ Je - sus, Lord, at Thy birth!

peace, Sleep_____ in hea - ven-ly peace.
born! Christ_____ the Sa - viour is born!
birth! Je - - - sus, Lord, at Thy birth!

peace, Sleep_ in heav'n - ly peace.
born! Christ_ the Sa - viour's born!
birth! Je - sus, Lord, Thy birth!

- ven-ly peace, Sleep_____ in hea - ven-ly peace.
- viour is born! Christ_____ the Sa - viour is born!
____ at Thy birth! Je - - sus, Lord, at Thy birth!

TENOR SOLO
(optional)

2. Si - lent night! ho - ly night!_ Shep - herds quake_____

4

at_____ the sight: Glo - ries stream_ from_ hea - ven a - far,_

7

Heav'n - ly hosts sing - ing_ Al - le-lu - ia: Christ_ the Sa - viour is_

10   gliss.

born!_____ Christ the_ Sa - viour____ is_ born!

14. Away in a manger

William J. Kirkpatrick, Charles H. Gabriel

WILLIAM J. KIRKPATRICK
arranged Antony Pitts

Verse 1 or verse 3 harmony may be used throughout.

2. The cat - tle are_ low - ing, the_ ba - by_ a - wakes,_ But_

Je - sus no_
lit - tle Lord_ Je - sus no cry - ing_ He_ makes._ I
Je - sus no

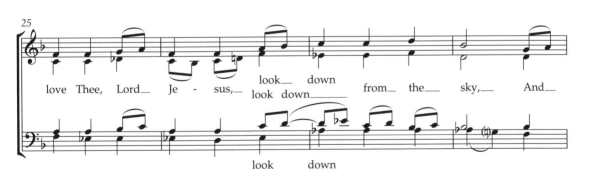

look_ down
love Thee, Lord_ Je - sus,_ look down__ from_ the_ sky,_ And_
look down

side un - til_
stay by my side un - til morn - ing is_ nigh._
stay_ by my side un - til morn - ing is nigh.

72

15. Baby Jesus, hush! now sleep

(after Czech Trad.)
Antony Pitts

TRAD. (CZECH)
arranged Antony Pitts

May be sung unaccompanied – hum cue notes as appropriate.

16. O little town of Bethlehem

Phillips Brooks

JOHN MICHAEL PITTS
arranged Antony Pitts

Verse 1 harmony; verse 2 unison; verse 3 harmony (unaccompanied);
if enough voices, verse 4 may be sung to both 4-part versions simultaneously.

8

A - bove thy deep and dream - less
And prais - es sing to God the
Cast out our sin, and en - ter

So God im - parts to hu - man
Cast out our sin, and en - ter

12

sleep The si - lent stars go by:
King, And peace to men on earth.
in: Be born in us to - day.

hearts The bless - ings of His heav'n.
in: Be born in us to - day.

80

17. Jesu, the very thought is sweet
(*O Jesulein süss*)

(*Jesu dulcis memoria*)
John M. Neale

17TH-CENTURY, figured J.S. BACH
realised Antony Pitts

1. Je - su!___ the___ ve - ry___ thought is___ sweet; In that___ dear Name___ all___ heart - joys meet; But___ oh!___ than ho - ney___ sweet - er___ far___ The___ glimps - es of___ His___ Pre - sence___ are.___ Je - su!___ the___ ve - ry___ thought___ is___ sweet.

2. No word is sung___ more sweet___ than this, No sound___ is heard___ more full___ of___ bliss, No___ thought brings sweet - er___ com - fort___ nigh,___ Than Je - sus, Son___ of___ God___ most High.___ No word___ is___ sung___ more sweet___ than this.

3. Je - su,___ the___ hope___ of___ souls___ for - lorn, How good___ to them___ for___ sin___ that___ mourn! To___ them___ that___ seek___ Thee, oh___ how___ kind!___ But___ what___ art Thou to them___ that___ find? Je - su,___ the___ hope___ of___ souls___ for - lorn.

Verse 6 may be omitted.

4. No tongue of mor-tal can ex-press, No pen can
5. O Je-su, King of won-drous might! O Vic-tor,
6. A-bide with us, O LORD, to-day, Ful-fil us

write the bless-ed-ness, He on-ly who hath
glo-rious from the fight! Sweet-ness that may not
with Thy grace we pray; And with Thine own true

proved it knows What bliss from love of Je-sus
be ex-press'd, And al-to-ge-ther love-li-
sweet-ness feed Our souls from sin and dark-ness

flows. No tongue of mor-tal can ex-press.
-est! O Je-su, King of won-drous might!
freed. A-bide with us, O LORD, to-day.

18. O come, all ye faithful

(after Anon.)
F. Oakeley

collected? JOHN FRANCIS WADE
arranged Antony Pitts

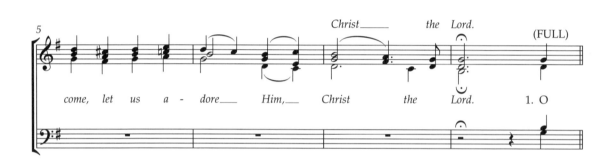

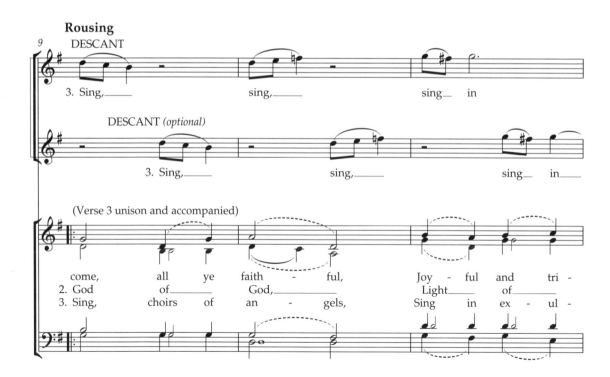

Verse 2 may be sung unaccompanied; preferably both descants should be sung in verse 3, spatially separated, and doubled on instruments as appropriate.

a - dore! a - dore! a - dore Him,

a - dore! a - dore! a -

-dore Him, O come let us a - dore Him, O come, let us a-

dore Him, O come, O come, o come a-

O come let us a - dore

Christ the Lord.

- dore Him, Christ the Lord.

-dore Him, Christ the Lord.

- dore Him, Christ the Lord.

Him, Christ the Lord.

ALL

4. Yea, Lord, we greet Thee, Born this hap - py morn - ing;

19. Personent hodie

Piae Cantiones (1582)

PIAE CANTIONES (1582)
arr. Antony Pitts

This carol may be sung unison or in harmony throughout – with or without organ descants; an ideal version is:
verse 1 TB unison (unaccompanied); verse 2 SA unison; verse 3 SATB harmony; verse 4 Full unison.

20. In dulci jubilo

14th-Century(?),
Valentin Triller, Antony Pitts

MICHAEL PRAETORIUS,
J.S. BACH, JOHN STAINER
arranged Antony Pitts

May be sung unison with accompaniment throughout.

21. Good King Wenceslas

John M. Neale

PIAE CANTIONES (1582)
arranged Antony Pitts

This carol is particularly suited to accompaniment on the piano.

98

32 S.A.
Fails my heart, I know not how: I can go no long - er."

34 T.B.
"Mark my foot - steps, good my page, Tread thou in them bold - ly:

36
Thou shalt find the win - ter's rage Freeze thy blood less cold - ly."

39 S.A.
5. In his mas - ter's steps he trod, Where the snow lay dint - ed;
T.B.

22. We three kings of Orient are

John Henry Hopkins

JOHN HENRY HOPKINS
arranged Antony Pitts

Verse 1 (original) harmony may be used throughout – with or without verse 5 descant.

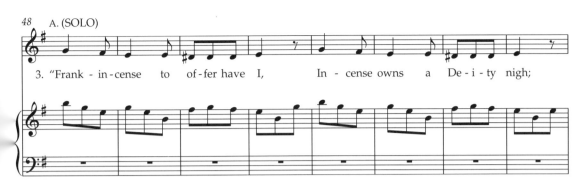

3. "Frank - in -cense to of -fer have I, In - cense owns a De - i - ty nigh;

Prayer and prais - ing all men rais - ing, Wor-ship Him, God most High."

repeat REFRAIN

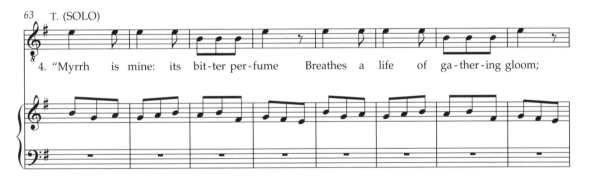

4. "Myrrh is mine: its bit-ter per-fume Breathes a life of ga -ther-ing gloom;

Sor-row-ing, sigh - ing, bleed - ing, dy - ing, Sealed in the stone - cold tomb."

repeat REFRAIN

106

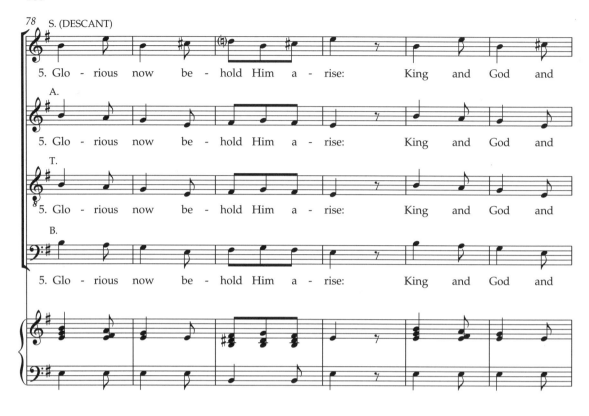

REFRAIN (last time)

-lu - ia" the earth___ re - plies. O_____

-lu - ia" the earth___ re - plies. O_____

-lu - ia" the earth___ re - plies. O_____

-lu - ia" the earth___ re - plies. O_____

star of won - der, star of night, Star with

star of won - der, star of night, Star with

star of won - der, star of night, Star with

star of won - der, star of night, Star with

23. I saw three ships come sailing in

Trad. (English)

TRAD. (ENGLISH)
arranged Antony Pitts

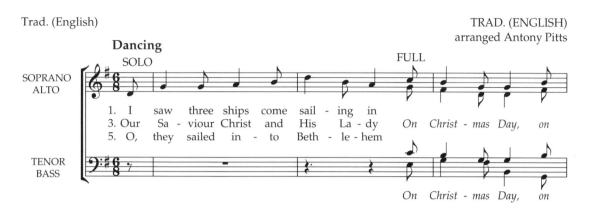

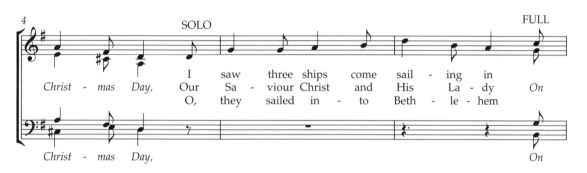

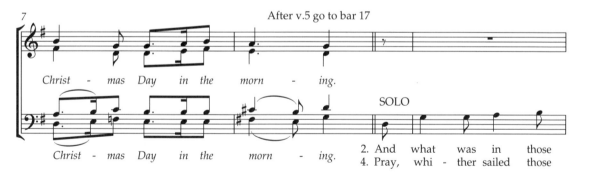

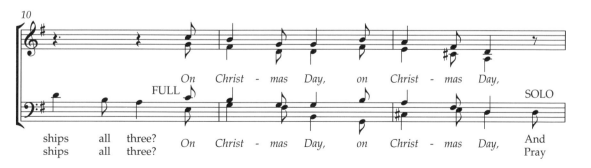

Verse 6 may be sung as three separate verses.

24. Hail to the Lord's Anointed

(after Psalm 72)
James Montgomery

ANTONY PITTS

May be sung to verse 2 harmony throughout – with optional verse 5 unison and organ harmony.

24

- y, And bid the weak be strong; To give them songs for sigh-ing, Their

- y, And bid the weak be strong; To give them songs for sigh-ing, Their

- y, And bid the weak be strong; To give them songs for sigh-ing, Their

- y, And bid the weak be strong; To give them songs for sigh-ing, Their

28

dark - ness turn to light, Whose souls, con - demned and

dark - ness turn to light, Whose souls, con - demned and

dark - ness turn to light, Whose souls, con - demned and

dark - ness turn to light, Whose souls, con - demned and

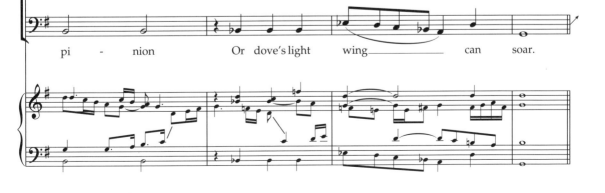